PENGUIN BOOKS

BURN LAKE

Carrie Fountain was born and raised in Mesilla, New Mexico. She was a fellow at the University of Texas's Michener Center for Writers. Her poems have appeared in *Crazyhorse*, *AGNI*, and *Southwestern American Literature*, among others. She lives in Austin, Texas, and teaches at St. Edward's University.

THE NATIONAL POETRY SERIES

The National Poetry Series was established in 1978 to ensure the publication of five poetry books annually through five participating publishers. Publication is funded by the Lannan Foundation, Stephen Graham, Joyce & Seward Johnson Foundation, Glenn and Renee Schaeffer, and Juliet Lea Hillman Simonds.

2009 Competition Winners

Julie Carr of Denver, Colorado, *Sarah—Of Fragments and Lines*
Chosen by Eileen Myles, to be published by Coffee House Press

Colin Cheney of Brooklyn, New York, *Here Be Monsters*
Chosen by David Wojahn, to be published by University of Georgia Press

Carrie Fountain of Austin, Texas, *Burn Lake*
Chosen by Natasha Trethewey, to be published by Penguin Books

Erika Meitner of Blacksburg, Virginia, *Ideal Cities*
Chosen by Paul Guest, to be published by HarperCollins Publishers

Jena Osman of Philadelphia, Pennsylvania, *The Network*
Chosen by Prageeta Sharma, to be published by Fence Books

BURN LAKE

Carrie Fountain

PENGUIN BOOKS

PENGUIN BOOKS

Published by the Penguin Group

Penguin Group (USA) Inc., 375 Hudson Street, New York, New York 10014, U.S.A.
Penguin Group (Canada), 90 Eglinton Avenue East, Suite 700, Toronto, Ontario, Canada M4P 2Y3
(a division of Pearson Penguin Canada Inc.)
Penguin Books Ltd, 80 Strand, London WC2R 0RL, England
Penguin Ireland, 25 St Stephen's Green, Dublin 2, Ireland (a division of Penguin Books Ltd)
Penguin Group (Australia), 250 Camberwell Road, Camberwell, Victoria 3124, Australia
(a division of Pearson Australia Group Pty Ltd)
Penguin Books India Pvt Ltd, 11 Community Centre, Panchsheel Park, New Delhi 110 017, India
Penguin Group (NZ), 67 Apollo Drive, Rosedale, North Shore 0632, New Zealand (a division of Pearson
New Zealand Ltd)
Penguin Books (South Africa) (Pty) Ltd, 24 Sturdee Avenue, Rosebank, Johannesburg 2196, South Africa

Penguin Books Ltd, Registered Offices:
80 Strand, London WC2R 0RL, England

First published in Penguin Books 2010

LIBRARY OF CONGRESS CATALOGING IN PUBLICATION DATA
Fountain, Carrie.
Burn Lake / Carrie Fountain.
p.   cm.   (National poetry series)
ISBN 978 0 14 311771 1
1. Title.
PS3606.O84425B87   2010
811'.6   dc22   2010008245

Set in Walbaum MT
Designed by Ginger Legato

For Kirk

ACKNOWLEDGMENTS

Some of these poems, a few with different titles, were first published in the following magazines and anthologies, to whose editors grateful acknowledgment is made:

32 Poems
AGNI
Ascent
Borderlands: Texas Poetry Review
Cave Wall
Cimarron Review
Crazyhorse
cream city review
Hayden's Ferry Review
Marlboro Review
The Missouri Review
Southwestern American Literature
Swink
The Texas Observer

"What" first appeared in *Is This Forever, or What?*, published by Greenwillow Books/HarperCollins in 2004.

"Lightning" appeared in *Between Heaven and Texas*, published by the University of Texas Press in 2006.

For support, my thanks to the Frank Waters Foundation and the James A. Michener Center for Writers. Thanks to Jim Magnuson in particular, for encouragement.

For help with this manuscript, my most sincere thanks to Marie Howe, Steve Moore, Amber Hall, Deb Paredez, Emily Forland, Carra Martinez, Vive Griffith, Jake Silverstein, Bruce

Snider, Dave Fruchter, and Phil Pardi. Thanks to Sam Suite
for those stamped envelopes. Thanks to Billie and Al Fountain.
My deepest gratitude to my teacher and friend Naomi Nye.
Finally, endless thanks and boundless love to my husband,
Kirk Lynn: *throughout.*

CONTENTS

III. In History

You are now on the
continent of the insatiate.

At least no one can deprive
you, even destitute, of that.

—HENRI MICHAUX

BURN LAKE

I. Experience

Experience

When I think of everything I've wanted
I feel sick. There was this one night in winter
when Jennifer Scanlon and I were driven out
to the desert to be the only girls there
when the boys got drunk and chose
the weakest among themselves to beat the living
shit out of again and again while the night
continued in its airy way to say nothing. Sure, I wanted
to believe violence was a little bell you could ring
and get what you wanted. It seemed to work for those
boys, who'd brought strict order to the evening
using nothing but a few enthusiastic muscles.
Even when he'd begun bleeding from his nose, the boy
stayed. It was an initiation. That's what he believed.
Thank God time keeps erasing everything in this steady,
impeccable way. Now it's like I never lived
that life, never had to, sitting on a tailgate
while Jennifer asked for advice on things she'd already done,
watching the stars ferment above, adoring whatever it was
that allowed those boys to throw themselves fists-first
at the world, yell every profanity ever made
into the open ear of the universe. I believed then
that if only they'd get quiet enough, we'd hear
the universe calling back, telling us what to do next.
Of course, if we'd been quiet, we would've heard
nothing. And that silence, too, would've ruined us.

Burn Lake

For Burn Construction Company

When you were building the I-10 bypass,
one of your dozers, moving earth
at the center of a great pit,
slipped its thick blade beneath
the water table, slicing into the earth's
wet palm, and the silt moistened
beneath the huge thing's tires, and the crew
was sent home for the day.
Next morning, water filled the pit.
Nothing anyone could do to stop it coming.
It was a revelation: kidney-shaped, deep
green, there between the interstate
and the sewage treatment plant.
When nothing else worked, you called it
a lake and opened it to the public.
And we were the public.

Starting Small

At sunset on the Fourth of July,
just as the Shriners began shooting
fireworks over the football stadium,

the first McDonald's in Las Cruces
switched on its lights and unlocked its doors
and shone there harshly

against the nothing, like a shrine
to itself, a prize we could claim.
And that same evening,

while my brother and I were waiting in line
to place our orders,
by some act of grace

the vacant lot across the street
caught fire, starting small,
then gaining, tossing everything—every tumbleweed
and paper cup—into its sack of flames.

We were children.

We'd walked three miles to get there.

We'd walked across the interstate
just like we said we wouldn't.

What a pleasure—
I'm tempted to say *what a relief*—
it was to see it: fire

dancing around in front of us
like a trained animal.

We ate our burgers on the sidewalk.

They were all right.

Behind us, in the sky,
the city of Las Cruces
was explaining its independence

the best way it knew how.

We knew very little, almost nothing,

though at some point that evening,
when the fire was at a peak
and the heat coming off it

made us squint from across the street,

my brother leaned in to me
and said, with the satisfaction of someone
who has won a long, ongoing argument,

"This is a miracle."

His mouth was an O
of grease and ketchup,

his cheeks red
with heat and admiration.

He looked—I'm tempted to say—
like an angel.

He looked like
he'd never recover.

The fire lifted its big,
meaty tongue as if to speak, then fell over
and kept burning.

It got late. We had to go.
We walked home along the ditch,
kicking each other, grown tired once again
of each other's company.

We grew up.

Something big was built
on that vacant lot, something
indestructible

that wasn't big enough
and was torn down
so something bigger

that would go immediately out of business
could take its place.

Now I see what he meant.

The miracle
wasn't the fire.

The miracle was no one
called the fire department,
no one thought to,

and the miracle was that, allowed
to continue, the fire grew,

caught up with itself
every few yards

and grew. And the miracle was

no one stopped it, and the miracle was

no one wanted to stop it.

El Camino Real

I take and seize tenancy and possession, real and actual,
civil and natural, one, two, and three times . . . without
excepting anything and without limitations.

—Spanish governor Juan de Oñate, upon reaching
the Rio Grande at El Paso del Norte, Ascension Day, 1598

This is how they made the New World:
every once in a while they stopped,
they tied two yucca stalks together
to make the sign of the cross, they prayed.
Silence answered them from all directions
for hundreds of miles. The silence
did not want to stop. If they found a tree
they nailed the cross to it,
and the wind took away the hammer's *thuck.*
Then the one in front took up again
the staff of the royal standard.
And they went on, bearing those
absurd yellow silks up through the valley
and on into the desert.

Oñate

"I see what you mean," I said last night
as I lay in the desert, dying
of thirst, after you came to me in my dream
and said, "Here, my son, take it,
it's yours now," then opened your fist
to show me that your palm was empty.
The visible world is a bad example.
It's a perfect specimen in a sealed jar.
To open it would be to ruin it.

Burn Lake 2

All afternoon I've been swimming out
to the deepest part of the lake
and sinking down as far as I can
because for a long time now
I've wanted to feel dead and alive
at the same time
and for whatever reason I believe
this is the way to do it. So far,
it's impossible to feel dead.
Instead, when I reach the cold sheets
of water toward the bottom of the lake
all the lights go on inside my body
and my legs pump, and before long
I see the determined lines the sun makes
on the surface of the water, and I reach
the living world again, the thin limbs
of the salt cedar wagging at the shoreline,
the *wuzz* of traffic on the interstate,
and my mother, far off, reading a paperback
on a little shelf of sand, smoking
one of those long, brown cigarettes
she slips in one sublime gesture
from out of a clicking leather case.
There is something that keeps
occurring to me in the moment I break
the water, though by the time I take a breath
I've forgotten what it was.

Theory of Fate

In that place, at that time,
the way it worked was

there came a moment—
maybe you brought it on yourself,
maybe not—

when you became the kind of person
you were meant to be.

It was simple.

If you were meant to be the kind of man
who'd hit a woman,

there'd come the moment—
the circumstances
wouldn't matter—

when you'd hit a woman
for the first time,

in the face or the neck
or the tender breast,

and the feeling of being
what you were meant to be
would settle upon you,

and you'd know
what to do or not do
to begin living life

that way, full of remorse
and shame or not,

and women would come to you
or stay away from you
or call the police
or murder you in your sleep,

depending
on the kind of person
they'd become.

This was the only way.

You were meant to drink; you'd drink.

You were meant to be found
one morning in a ditch
with your pants around your ankles
and your mouth full of mud,

and there you were.

If you were meant to be a bystander—
If you were meant to die young—
If you were meant to be born again—

At that time, in that place
this was the prevailing theory.

And this is the information
I was going on

the day I slipped behind the bar,
where just around the corner
my father

was selling his regrets to the world
in the late afternoon heat,

and I swiped a cigar for me
and the girl next door
to choke on behind the post office.

Any second my father could've
rounded the corner and caught me

stealing from him.
Yet there I was, taking it.

What

"Is this forever, or what?" I asked
a few weeks into the summer.
The sky had widened, and I needed to know
right then, while we were parked
in the lot behind the waterslide
where nothing grew, just us
and dust, and our little city buzzed
in the valley, a dozen or so roads
cut into it. It'd be nice to go back
to speaking so easily. "Just ask,"
the sky suggested. And in response,
the boy turned the key in the ignition
and drove us back to town, along
those same streets, which led one
into the next and were not measured
until we'd passed over them.

The Change

I swear the year my mother
stopped having her period
was the same year I started

having sex, the year
I spent my evenings
parked by the river, getting good

at revealing my breasts
to my sensitive boyfriend,
my ass, my armpits, learning

the idiom of his body
as well: the slight, stern curve
of the man's waist, the slope

of the shoulders, the comic
sag of the testicles; learning
the feel of sex, painful

and reassuring, as if the two of us
were slowly being sewn
together while my mother

was going away, to be sad
beyond the capacity
of her heart because the time

of her life had commenced
to dry and harden, like stucco
against the walls of her body.

And didn't she start to shrink?
I think so. In fact, I think
she began to disappear

that fall, from the face
of the earth, though I didn't
really notice

and wouldn't notice
and had made a high
art out of not noticing.

I didn't like talking to her.
Her dust-colored bangs
had a tendency to fall

with absolutely no grace
into her gray eyes,
and I couldn't bear to see her

push them, again
and again, out of the way.
She was her own

planet by then.
One afternoon in winter
she came to my bedroom door

holding a fistful of tampons,
standing there in the doorway
holding them out to me,

her mouth saying jovially,
"I guess I don't need
these things anymore,"

though by the time
the sound reached me
from those many light-years

away, what I heard was,
"Take them, you fool, and run
for your life."

Warnings from the Window

Look out there: Altie
has taken his soccer ball
out to the acres, is kicking around
once again in the onions.
Who could tell him
tomorrow's the day
the men move in, fill their trucks,
and leave the field pocked,
the road rutted? He's so young:
towheaded and in love
with his feet. One moment
and the sun will loosen
in its socket. The sky
will clench like a fist to catch it.
The boy will look up, suddenly
distracted by the gruff sound
of traffic on the highway
beyond the field. Interstate 10.
Florida to California. Out
bound, outgoing.
Look, the boy is bending at the waist
to tie his shoe. The real work
of living begins. The window
whispers, *Here it comes,*
ahead, away.

Restaurant Fire, Truth or Consequences

We stood on the curb after dinner and watched the black smoke
pour from the drive-through window, the flames doing their steady work
behind the counter while the employees chatted nervously
in the parking lot, holding their personal belongings.
We watched until the breeze shifted and the smoke began inching
toward us, and then we walked to the car and drove home.
My guess is we'll never mention it again, not once, as long as we live.
This morning I woke early, feeling industrious. Another week
inched open. I know there's no going back to look at that fire, no matter
how little I desire to do so. And that is the precise heartbreak
of the past: that it doesn't return, not even when you don't want it to.

The Continental Divide

"Let me see if I understand you
correctly." Those were the only words
I could beg from my guts

in asking him to explain the feelings
he'd waited

until we'd made it to the top of this mountain
to admit he was no longer having for me.

He explained. And while he explained,
I could feel the handful of air I'd coerced
into my body begin to escape,

as if I'd been pricked, and there, among
the cold top rocks

at the summit,
I thought of crying.

I thought of crying
in an abstract way; I thought of
really going for it—letting loose, crying

so much a little river of tears
would spring up
beneath our boots; and I wondered then

which side of America
a river of tears would choose, wondered
what it was that made me feel
not like he was leaving me

but like he was stealing from me,
like he'd been stealing from me

the whole time, ripping me off a little
each day, dipping his fingers

into my private stash—of what?
It didn't matter. Only

that he'd taken it.

I felt the sloped
chest-bone of the country
begin to crack in two.

No such luck. The earth stayed
where it was, out of reach, and over

the dashboard, on the way back to town,
one tired fly hit and re-hit the windshield

in pursuit of the opening
that would allow it to return

to the huge, blue night.
As if that opening

was inevitable. As if flinging one's body against something
over and over again
ever got anyone anywhere.

I wished then
to find some plant off the side of the road
I could stare at

while the formula for pain
was proving itself throughout my body, one bush

under which I could dig a neat hole
and empty the shredded documents
from my rib cage, a hole

to which I could return in fall, to dig them up
and sort them out. I wished to find one
supple pine into the shin of which I could inject

my vial full—of what?

It didn't matter. Only that
I might relieve the ache. No matter
if the tree
slumped over and died.

No matter trees around the world
are sick to death of pain
and metaphor, our underwear

slung into the high branches,
our forests dry, our desert floors

soaked, not with our blood,
but with the blood of those
with whom we felt
it just wasn't going to work.

Columbus, toeing the coast of San Salvador,
never went down on his knee
and thanked God.

He'd reached paradise!

He went to his ledger, tongued
his pen, and started working with the figures.

Gold, blood, love: what we call natural
we are in truth calling available.

And when we say available

we usually mean taken.

We were simply an example. "Love,"
we said, and planted our flag, and took stock
of our natural resources.

Then the bottom fell out
of the economy, and I was left

carrying fistfuls of bills that meant
nothing, could buy me
nothing.

I wished to be healed,
and I wasn't healed.

I wished to be compensated.
I wasn't compensated.

So then I wished I could simply forget
my time in that large

and violent country; I wished
I could go back

in a snappy little boat
to my homeland.

But there was no more ocean. There was
no going back. There was only

inland, the woods, and beyond
the woods, God only knows.

Theory of Perfection

It smells like asphalt
and air, a distance so great
you'd evaporate
long before arriving there.

It's a kind of haunting.
When you sink
to the bottom
of a swimming pool
and lay your cheek
against the floor

and imagine yourself
unimagined,

it's that big, clogged
silence that sends you back
to the surface, to the air.

It looks so hard.
Like the way, with all of us
watching, the woman

who taught etiquette classes
in a strip mall in Las Cruces

showed us one night
how a lady picks up
a dropped pen;

how she sidled up to it,
as if doing so was an act
of nonviolent resistance,

and then sort of collapsed
at the knees

so it seemed certain
for one long moment

that her existence—that all
of existence—was resting

there, bottom-heavy
and sad, on her slim
and attractive ankles.

And how she snatched
the pen up.

And how she threw it down
again, so that, one by one,
we girls

would have a chance
to practice.

Heaven

We spent months of our lives walking
from Sears to Penney's, back when we were
vague, a couple of ideas forming ourselves
against the certainty of merchandise,
in the presence of strangers, when no one
knew us or wished to know us or could even
perceive us as we passed, two girls, unsmiling,
unwilling, not finished. When I think
of what we looked like then I think
of newborn horses: stunned and exhausted,
still slick with the cumbersome fluids of birth.
You were the leader. You'd stop
at the waterfall by the food court, dig a coin
from your pocket, and toss it over your shoulder
into the fiberglass river, then turn, press a coin
into my palm, and say, "Now you do it."
We were hopeful. Our quarters slapped the water
and disappeared beneath it. The little river
went on, past the shoe store. And we followed it—
we followed it as long as we could, longing
toward this: the unseen, unwished-for present.

II. Progress

Want

The wasps outside
the kitchen window
are making that
thick, unraveling sound
again, floating in
and out of the bald head
of their nest,
seeming not to move
while moving,
and it has just occurred
to me, standing,
washing the coffeepot,
watching them hang
loosely in the air—thin
wings; thick, elongated
abdomens; sad, down-
pointing antennae—
that this
is the heart's constant
project: this simple
learning; learning
how to hold
hopelessness
and hope together;
to see on the unharmed
surface of one
the great scar
of the other; to recognize
both and to make

something of both;
to desire everything
and nothing
at once and to desire it
all the time;
and to contain that desire
fleshly, in a body;
to wash it and rest it
and feed it; to learn
its name and from whence
it came; and to speak
to it—oh, most of all
to speak to it—
every day, every day,
saying to one part,
"Well, maybe this is all
you get," while saying
to the other, "Go on,
break it open, let it go."

Tonight the Neighbors Spell JESUS on Their Lawn in Christmas Lights

Walking by tonight, we're reminded
there must've been a first time
for everything—one green shoot, a drop
of bluish water, a few red cells.
The letters wink at us as if they know
what they're for, and we go by, saying,
"Oh God, look at that," as if we did, too.

Mornings, the lights are left on
to call very palely to the large,
uninterested sky. "We are all alone,"
they cry. And the sky answers back
by not moving an inch.

Summer Practice

The long, mellow hallway of spring has led to this:
it's massive July; it's seven thirty in the morning,
and someone down the street is shooting off bottle rockets.

The dog noses open the door to my study, drops to the floor, faces
the window. After each brief whistle there's a moment,
then a pop, and she scrambles again to her feet. When I lean down

and put my hand on her forehead, she drops once again to the floor,
exhaling deeply, as if she's disappointed with herself, as if
she has been trying to teach herself a skill her animal body

won't allow her to learn. The morning is turning over.
Soon the ice cream truck will be circling the block, tinking out
its heat-wobbly confusion of tunes: "Turkey in the Straw," "The Entertainer,"

"Silent Night." Prayer was the last skill I learned. I practiced
rigorously. Just as I was getting good, I lost it. As soon as it
was gone, I understood it was not a skill at all.

lightning

The sky's cranked up
all the way, huge and blue
as it's going to get.

He's around back, doing
something up a ladder.
She's just come home

and is talking about work,
purse dangling from her wrist.
Sometimes she gets the sense

he's pretending not to listen
to her. Not ignoring her,
but pretending not to listen.

But he's not. He's always
listening to her. Sometimes
he thinks she must be

bored with him.
Later, when they tell this story,
they'll mention the nearly

cloudless sky, the weird smell
like burnt hair when the rock
cracked cleanly in two, how

she fell onto the lawn. They'll say
it came out of nowhere and was loud
and bright as hell.

Progress

When they paved the streets of Mesilla,
they dug a trench in front of our house, four feet
wide, three feet deep, where the sidewalk
would eventually go, and my father
laid a steel plate across it
so he could pull his car into the drive—
come and go, come and go, which is what
he did—and my brother spent the rest
of that summer in the trench, under the plate,
alone down there in the silt and shade,
finding out what he was. I'd sit
on the porch pretending to read a book
while I watched those men from the city
in their plain blue shirts or not, the knuckles
of their work gloves thickly clotted with tar.
They returned every morning, clean as the sun,
with their bent, black shovels and that drum
of weeping tar. Every day they made a little
progress. We were really getting somewhere.
A road is the crudest faith in things to come.

Rio Grande

Two brothers, a first-grader
and a fifth-grader, drowned
in the riptides last summer,
one slipping under and the other
going in to save him.
In September, the school
held a ceremony out front,
and the student council president,
a lean girl in a blue dress,
with tanned forearms and hair held back
in a smart ponytail, presented
the boys' mother with the two
bronze plaques that would sit
at the feet of the sapling firs
already planted in their remembrance
beside the squat adobe building.
The boys' mother handed
her daughter to her husband
and took the plaques, one in each
hand, and stood holding them
while the entire student body,
the teachers, and the principal
in his tweed sport coat stared
into the dark argument of her face.
They were taken, the plaques
say, or something like that.
Now it's spring again. The river
is filling with water from far away,

cold water from the Rockies, the snows
melting, falling, simple, pulled
down the continent like a zipper.

Oñate 2

Praise God, we've found
the river again; we're back
tonight at the lip of wanting,

having lost many of our party
passing through the place
called Jornada del Muerto.

We drank all we could,
then lay on the banks, swollen
as toads, looking up

into the cottonwoods, filled
with that great discomfort,
able only to roll over

every once in a while
to undo our pants
and piss.

Though we warned them
against it, two men allowed
their horses too much

pleasure, and the mares
drank so much
their stomachs burst,

and they died standing up
in the river, and their hulking
bodies were taken

very slowly away,
downstream, back, I told
the men to console them,

to the great ocean
that bore our Christ to this new
and terrible continent.

The friars blessed the journey.
We ate and then we slept.
Late at night, I woke

from a bad dream.
When I regained my faculties
I went to stand at the river.

The water was busy
pursuing its own ending.
The moon,

on the other hand, was just
hanging there, unclaimed, milk
that would go bad. So I drank it.

The Groom

I'm going back one more time to look for my mother's ring, the one
from her first marriage, to a man named Gordon, a man we never even
saw a photo of, the ring the only proof we ever found of her first life, the ring
I took from her jewelry box and lost during a wedding ceremony
in the cactus garden behind the house, practicing that one dumb ritual
of adulthood with Liz. When I told my mother I'd looked everywhere,
she blinked softly once. If she'd been a more decisive person,
she'd have hit me. Instead, what she said was, "Don't tell your father."
I'm going back one more time to that day, just to look around:
it isn't my turn to be the bride. I part my hair and wear my brother's shoes
and wait amidst the cholla, the ocotillo, the ring warming in my pocket
while my bride glides toward me, making her slow way through the thorns,
which we understand to be highly formal, her small face unseen, untouched,
hidden behind a lace pillowcase. By the time she gets to me, I've lost it.

Late Summer

Out for a walk tonight,
the dog is throwing all her weight
against the leash, lunging toward
the fat tomcat

licking his black ankles
with a delicious, solemn attention
at the top of the neighbor's steps.

Because this is what the dog
was made to do.
Because for some lucky animals

the space between the body
and what it wants
is all there is.

Mother and Daughter at the Mesilla Valley Mall

She's learning to walk
through department stores

with her mother so it looks like
they aren't together.

There's a technique to it
that involves browsing

and yawning, her hesitant body
pulled from rack to rack

by the bored points
of her thin hips, the drone

of the air conditioner—the one
proof of a universe—churning

just above the low ceiling.
She can't be more than

fourteen, fingers working
nimbly through the T-shirts

while her mother waits, lips
pursed, at a distance,

for her daughter to choose
something, anything:

TODAY ONLY, the signs read,
HALF OFF EVERYTHING!

What do you think it would take
for this girl to, say, touch

her mother's hand
as they wait for the elevator,

or as they step into it, as it takes them
to the next level, where the girl

will get lost again, as soon as she can,
among the shoes and scarves

and gowns and umbrellas? I think
it would take more than she has. Her whole

body says, "Please, don't expect much,"
when a moment later her mother

comes to her with a dress
made almost purely

of pearls and silver sequins,
holds it to her daughter's frame,

and says, "You'd look beautiful
in this one." *Beautiful*: a word

so poorly built. How does it
stand up? The woman's face

surrenders, her mouth
goes soft and slack.

I won't tell you
what the girl says back.

If Your Mother Was to Tell Your Life Story

It would start with her.

It could learn to tie a knot; you would be bound to it.

It would stink and she'd win.

It'd be nice to know.

Once and for all.

The mellow swings behind the house.

The many lives of the cactus garden.

It wouldn't know where to start.

It wouldn't even know the half of it.

It wouldn't know that she was a country, that you'd pledged your allegiance to her.

It wouldn't know there'd been a war.

It would forget everything.

It would get things so wrong it wouldn't even be funny.

It would be funny.

It would be shrewd.

It would delight her, wouldn't it?

Oh, those little armies. How they'd perished.

Her thirties, her forties, her fifties.

Her heart, her heart: lick of flame, little fish.

It could leave you behind.

It could take you away.

It would be hers. And it would be yours.

And then it would be hers again.

Getting Better

When his acne began to clear up,
my brother put on new cleats
and played one last year
of varsity football, his face
deeply scarred, running the field
with a rage people watching
could ease back in their seats
and fall in love with.
Resting, he'd bend at the waist,
hands on his knees, and suck
at the air like it was the enemy.
And in this way the days
of not knowing if things
were getting better or worse—
those days of waiting
for the storm of hormones
to pass—grew short and cold
until they were gone entirely
and he could begin forgetting them,
one by unforgettable one.
Of course, I could tell you everything
my brother has forgotten
about those bad years: the metallic smell
of his breath, how he became
meticulous about his clothing,
waking early to iron starch
into his T-shirts, how he'd plan
and execute small acts of violence,
once killing all my mother's

houseplants by pulling them up,
snipping their roots with a pair
of kitchen scissors, and then
sticking them back in the soil.
All he had then was tidiness
and cruelty, and he favored cruelty.
It was his last, dulled weapon—a hatchet
whose blade couldn't kill with one
blow, but could abuse, nonetheless,
to death, and I watched him use it
with great fear and interest.
I was his witness. Let me tell you
how the field mouse looked
when I pried open the can
of house paint to find it writhing there,
dying, eyes coated, face coated, mouth
opening and closing, and how
my brother had suddenly seemed
so lovely, so calm, as if he'd just
landed, handing the can to me,
saying, "Open it. Just open it."

Thrift

My father was a bartender; he came home
late and heavy, with a jar full of tips.
Mornings, my mother counted the change,
rolled it, hid it. From whom?
Never mind. It was a fortune, she said.
It was becoming a fortune. Mornings,
the desert cracked, the sun rose.
When it got dark my father reheated
a cup of coffee, drank it, brushed his teeth
over the kitchen sink, tied his shoes,
and went to work. My mother
sometimes painted her toenails
a color called Oh Mercy Me! It was the color
of blood diluted in water, the color
of the water in the jar after the last
of the maraschino cherries were gone,
before my father rinsed it, dried it,
set it out on the bar.

I-25

I'm never going to be in love with the boy
who thinks he's always going to be in love
with me, who thinks it's a good idea
to sneak out of his house in the middle
of the night and throw little pebbles, one
by one, then handfuls of gravel, handful
by handful, then single, thunder-loud rocks
at my mother's window, thinking it's mine.
That night, my mother will come crawling
into my bedroom on her hands and knees,
like an animal, her breasts swinging loosely
inside her flannel nightshirt, sidling up
to my bed, asking, "Do you hear that?"
She will ask, "Who is it?" She will beg.
She'll beg and I'll know, but I won't say,
will never say, not when her window cracks,
not when his muffler rumbles up and goes off,
toward the 10, insinuating itself back into
the various hums of the night, not when she pulls me
out of my bed, to the floor, against her chest,
yelling, "What did they want, goddamn it?
Was it you?" She will call into my face
late into that night, and for many nights
to come she will call and she will call,
but I won't hear her, and I won't hear her
because I'll be in that goddamn car with that
goddamn boy, and we'll be on the highway,
and we'll be halfway around the world.

The Coast

If in the said provinces, any seaports should be found on the
North Sea . . . you shall notify the viceroy of New Spain,
telling him the news and giving an accurate report of the
configuration of the coast and the capacity of each harbor.

—Viceroy Luis de Velasco to Juan de Oñate, as Oñate
set out from Mexico City to the so-called province of
New Mexico, October 21, 1595

Like anything imagined, it goes on forever
if you want it to go on forever.

If you want it to be just over the horizon,
you'll keep seeing, in the waves of hot air

coming up from the desert floor,
the bright blue grimace of the ocean.

Last night, after falling asleep reading
the tedious and turgid documents

of the Coronado expedition, I woke
and didn't know anything about myself.

My life came back in rivulets: the red
couch in my office, the dog on her bed,

looking up now, and, behind all that,
a big, dim memory: the New Year's Eve

Liz and I snuck out of our beds and walked
the few blocks to my father's bar

and, through the dark windows, saw
our parents existing in there without us, weird

and sexual, my mother with a peacock feather
in her hair, her full breasts lit by the face

of the jukebox. It was after midnight.
Someone was going around

popping balloons with a lit cigarette.
We watched for a long time. We watched

and watched, and then we walked home
under the black winter sky, and the new year

opened its mouth and swallowed us.
What I'd thought we'd find there, we hadn't found.

Now, when I remember my mother leaning up
against the jukebox like that, thirty-five, maybe

forty, wearing a yellow sweater, a loose perm
on her head, though I know it didn't happen

this way, I can't help but remember
that she turned and looked, squinting through

the low windows, and, seeing me
there, swung her whole body around, hips-

first, as if to let me get a better look at her.
When I woke, the dog stood up, startled, and the book

fell closed in my lap. On the cover, a colorful image
of a fat priest blessing Indians in the desert.

The image is so crude. Hard to tell who believes this
is the beginning and who believes this is the end.

El Camino Real 2

*Caravans left the comparative ease of the Rio Grande River
at Points of Rocks, north of Las Cruces, and prepared for a
brutal, three-day march with little rest and no water.*

—Sally Bickley, *Jornada del Muerto: 90 Miles of Hell*

In the dead summer
of 1598, midway through
the Jornada del Muerto,
where the river turned away
and went off into terrain
too rough for the horses,
after he and his column
had exhausted the last
of their supplies but before
they came to the place
they'd call Socorro, before
the pueblo there
sent runners with water
and sweet corn
to save them, Don Juan
de Oñate, sweating to death
in his chaps and iron chest plate,
thought, "After this
suffering, if we survive this
suffering, we'll be there;
we'll walk into the open hands
of the sea."
And in his mind
he began once again

to compose the letter
to the viceroy,
which, one had to assume,
would find its way
to the king: *Dear Sirs,*
We're here.
The coast is very much
as I'd imagined it:
water indefinitely, empty
and ours.

Burn Lake 3

We found a duck, a mallard, dead
on the shore, head split, eyes loose,

yet when someone poked it with a stick
it shuddered suddenly

and stood up, then collapsed again
and died for real,
which to me explained a lot.

For a while I'd had a vague idea
I could kill myself by holding my breath.

Yet when I locked myself in my room
and tried it, I fainted, fell face-first

into the closet. I came to in a panic,
thinking for a moment
that I'd done it, and that death

was still just my little blue room
at the back of the house,
my brother's stereo thumping in the bathroom
while he toiled over his pornography.

I was shocked then
by my body, its plain intention to continue

with or without me,
and I'm still shocked by it. Every day now
I feel myself pressed harder into this life.

Sometimes it's so near and docile
I can feel my hand take hold of it.

Other times it's that old, alarming
sorrow, that animal scrambling

to its feet, desperate

to be living.

Because it's mine, I wait for it to die.
Then I bury it.

Aubade at Bosque Redondo

Almost nothing has changed
about the world. We're still bound
to go on having this hunch

everything has left us or is waiting
for the worst possible moment to do so.
It's still our custom as a people

to measure our lives by our longing,
our longing by our treasure, our treasure
by the little pieces of jewelry

we let slip out of our hands
and clink down the drain, gone forever.
The prevailing theory is that if we try

hard enough an entire history
of diamond stud earrings will gurgle
forth, as lonely for us as we are for them.

The airplanes of America disembark.
The passengers look up, sensing the first
inch toward that next city.

III. In History

San Ysidro, Doña Ana County

For there behind the kneeling figure of Ysidro ... was a
yolk of milk-white oxen. Holding the plow ... was a winged
angel wearing a golden surcoat.

—Peter Hurd, San Patricio, 1967

Imagine that first one dropping
from the sky: the hinged eye,

the latch, the watery wings.
Ysidro, tired, trailing his clumsy
oxen, looked up ...

In these kinds of stories, people
are always falling to their knees,

struck to the earth by the sudden
knowledge of their lives,
their own living flesh, the small
labor of their breath, continuing.

Shouldn't we all receive a god
this obvious? And then
again, don't we, in the end?

Ysidro fell to his knees, thankful.
Then, not quite sure
what to do next, he rose again
and picked up his whip.

Jornada del Muerto

I'd never been inside a Protestant church.
Everything there was made of friendliness;
the air was clear and tasteless. Someone

had leaned your electric guitar against
the casket, which seemed to me the cruelest
kind of joke. Beneath the pews, the air-

conditioning picked up the hem of my dress
and held it for a moment, above my ankle.
The sun pouring in through the windows

was agony and time and Christ's great
sacrifice, which seemed so much more doable
among the Methodists. Everything said *continue*

or die, your choice. And that was the grief
that dazzled: knowing there are things
that should destroy us that don't destroy us.

Late Spring in the Mesilla Valley

Walking this morning,
I thought, What if I stop saying
the little no I'm always saying?
What if I drop it right here
in the middle of Rabb Road?
You know the guy down the street
who left his Christmas lights up
until after Easter? Well, did you see
all the odd little mirrors he hung
in the bushes alongside his house?
I keep thinking I'd like to be forced
into a conversation with yes.
It's not enough to brace yourself;
eventually you must allow this world
to hit you in the face.
All night I've been getting whiffs
of some late-blooming honeysuckle.
Half of me says, *Don't breathe.*
But only half.

Ordinary Sadness

It's simple, like sugar-water, like the shadow
cast by the banana, which was an eager yellow yesterday
but went bad overnight on the counter.
It comes from us. Evenings, my father walked
the perimeter of the pecan orchard, thinking for hours
about everything he'd never done. He was inconsolable.
And I was a teenager, grasping at happiness
and getting some, my body helping, until I simply
couldn't be talked out of my share, and I took it,
I stole it, like the one cigarette I was always stealing
from my mother's pack before slinking out
the back door, thinking, *Fuck that, man*, and heading
down the road, toward the lit center of town.

Father and Son at the Mesilla Valley Drive-thru Bank

It's a late Friday afternoon. The sky
is making that colossal pink gesture
that often precedes the dark.

The car in front of them finally pulls forward,
and the boy's father feeds the zipped bag of money
to the open mouth of the building.

From behind the glass, the woman speaks
into a long, thin microphone. She's so close,
if it weren't for the glass, she could lean over

and touch the roof of the car.
"This will only take a moment," she says,
smiling broadly.

Then, as if she'd disappeared entirely
from their view, she licks her thumb
and begins, without mercy, to count the bills.

Embarrassment

That afternoon,
while my parents and hers were inside
using the Super Bowl as an excuse
to get drunk in the middle of the day,
I locked my best friend and myself
inside the trunk of a car
for reasons I can't remember now.
I believe I was trying to prove a point.
After a few minutes,
when we realized there was no way out,
the air got hot and personal.
Our lives thrashed in us like rodents.
Yet, what I remember most
about the incident now
was the great, dawning sense
of just how stupid the situation
would seem to other people
if we died, how in a few hours
we could be some story
on the El Paso news, our parents
getting sober on TV, our bodies
laid on steel beds at the morgue,
naked, imperfect, irrevocably
embarrassed. How, in the beginning,
we laughed until we thought
we'd die laughing, and then stopped
suddenly, because we thought
we'd die, and then just lay there
crumpled into each other

like folding chairs and wept.
It was humiliating.
And an hour later,
when the trunk wheezed open
and my father was standing there
in his Chicago Bears jersey,
my mother behind him, her coat
folded smartly over her arm,
it was even more humiliating.
They didn't seem surprised
to find us there, turning blue,
or particularly angry,
though they did appear concerned.
"My God," they were saying, "my God."
Behind their heads, the pale
winter evening was waiting
like a pile of bones to be acknowledged.
Oh, I wanted to explain.
I wanted to start from the beginning
and account for each moment.
But I could do nothing
but breathe. My lungs
took all they could. My life was a bird
on a branch. There it was.
I saw it, looking down at me
with its unfocused eye
from just above my mother's head.
Oh, it wasn't beautiful.
But I knew better than to hate it.

Rio Grande 2

New Year's morning and the river is dry.
A refrigerator dumped there last summer
or the summer before is exposed again,
having not vanished into the good earth,
having not been taken back into
the earth's good hands. This morning
the Baptists across the street took down
the OUR SAVIOR IS BORN banner
above their door. It took two men
to roll the thing up, tie it on either end
with twine, and haul it to the shed
behind the building, where it will sit
another year, propped in a corner,
meaning almost nothing.

Burn Lake 4

One summer this pilot,
a Vietnam vet,

started taking tourists
for rides over town

in a glider. Every few hours
the tow-plane's old engine

ripped the sky in two.
Our city was nothing

much—"Nothing
to write home about,"

my mother would say
in her offhand way, moving

from sink to stove to table—
just a few hundred

buildings pressed
into the shoulders

of the desert, a highway
leading in and out.

One summer, and then
the business failed

and who knows
what happened

to the pilot and the plane
and the silent

little glider, its miraculous
underbelly, its elegant fin.

Childhood is like that
to a large extent,

isn't it? An ongoing lesson
in physics and disappointment.

Afternoons, floating
on my back, bored

with floating on my back,
I'd watch the glider

make its careful circles
against the rude curve

of the earth, the lake
under me. I wanted

to be seen just as much
as I didn't.

Purple Heart

In History, Beverly is showing me
a bruise on the inside of her arm;
she taps my shoulder each time the teacher
turns to write on the board
so she can point out another one
of its many features: yellowed edges, dead
center, blue spots, red. "That's blood,"
she whispers, "all of it." And the war
goes on for a few more minutes, the click
and drag of chalk on the board
as the Vietcong retreat again to the jungle
and the class grows more restless, little
conversations and flirtations springing up
everywhere, until suddenly our teacher,
overcome by our inattention, draws one
incredible breath, turns and writes
FUCK IT on the board, pulls her keys
from a drawer, unhooks one and lets it
drop—*clink*—to the floor, then walks down
the little aisle our desks make, looking no one
in the face, until she's out of the room, gone
forever, and one of us has to buzz the office.
Who knows? Who knows it will be Beverly
who will rise out of the silence and take charge,
calling each of us to her: the stunned;
the crying; the boy who takes the key
to the window and throws the goddamn thing
into the parking lot; the few
who are taking advantage of this time; the few

who are waiting, dumbstruck, for some
order, for anything, even if it's simply for that
horrible woman to come back, to continue
the lesson; the unchanged; the seemingly
unchanged; the changed; those who'll die
young; those who will go on in this world
to the eighth grade, to graduate, to investigate
their interests and exploit their potential,
to buy and sell, to make payments, to settle in.
When she pushes the button, the secretary
will say, "Yes?" from a thousand miles away,
and Beverly will say, "Something violent
happened here," she among us
understanding this is one way
the violent get you: not by coming
for you, but by leaving you behind.

I-10

Nights, I'd lie wrapped in my sheets and watch the westbound lanes
of the interstate make a horizon of headlights, rising over the hill
at the KOA sign and then disappearing, eventually, over the real horizon.
Even at three, four a.m., those real lives could be seen speeding
toward the blue eye of California. In late summer, the onions in the field
below my window pushed themselves up and out of the earth.
They'd shed their dead, outer skins, even while, inside, their wet,
white hearts were still dumbly growing.

Mesilla

Occasionally, I'd wake to the sound of a hot air balloon passing over the house, a short snarl of flame followed by a long, cool gap of silence. And once, while everyone was still sleeping, I got on my bike and followed to where one landed in a field across the highway, where I stood on the ditch and watched the huge, austere bulb touch down and the passengers, a boy and his father, climb out of the basket and the crew deflate the envelope; where after an hour or so, just as I'd hoped—just as I'd been hoping—someone called me over to help fold the fabric. It was nothing like I thought it'd be. It was a lot of waiting and then being spoken to brusquely by men who were not my father. It did bring about a great feeling of neatness, though, watching the enormous thing folded and folded and folded again, until it fit, impossibly, along with the cooled burners, into its own basket, which was hoisted onto a truck and driven away. Couldn't we be accounted for in the same way? Didn't we, too, carry our whole lives in our mouths?

Correcting the Metaphor

For a long time you thought it was a rope,
something you could use to pull
all of existence toward you, when really

it was a train inching across a wide horizon,
a train you couldn't see, no matter how much
you longed to, because, as it turned out,

you were inside it. You were inside
the train, and there were others: eager
faces, chatter, the wafting smells

of spices, perfume, ointments
and alcohol. You kept your forehead
to the window, looking out for a sign.

One morning, on top of a hill, you saw
a shepherd, surrounded by his flock,
standing with his back to you.

You imagined he was watching another train
crossing the next horizon. That's where
you made your mistake.

Socorro

I was renting a house that belonged to a woman I didn't know who had Alzheimer's and had gone to a rest home in Santa Fe. In the big front window her daughter had labeled the view: "Your pond," she'd written on an index card, "and your horses grazing beside it." Mornings, I'd go to the window. The horses would be down there, grazing beside the pond. Aside from their incremental movements, the earth was triumphantly still. I wondered what would happen to them when the woman died, though after a month or so a man came to the house and told me the pond was not actually on the woman's property, that I wasn't to swim or fish in it, and that the horses belonged to another man who lived up the road. That other man came one evening in late fall, loaded the horses into a trailer, and drove them away. The pond looked ludicrous by itself. Every few weeks an older couple came and fished it, pulling out great numbers of fish. The man tossed the fish he caught into his cooler; the woman smacked the fish against a rock a few times before doing the same. One morning I walked to the pond in the dark with a rod I'd chosen from many I found in the garage. I'd fished before, but I'd never caught anything. In fact, it hadn't occurred to me what I'd do with a fish until I felt the first pull.

Burn Lake 5

Afternoons, we swim to the far shore, where the broken bottles are, where Interstate 10 leans its great hip against the lake, and we watch the cars blow out of town, and we talk about the future.

We know about hope, swift and dangerous hope—everyone tip-toeing their way behind it, trying to grab it quick and tight behind its fanged head.

After high school, Daniel will spend two years mopping floors at the hospital, trying to decide whether to join the navy. Then one night he'll ride his motorcycle out of this world, and they'll find his body months later, at the bottom of Burn Lake.

The highway drags its black tail out of town. Things come and go.

We each keep an untouched life beneath the one we've been given.

Oñate 3

When we arrived at the place we called Socorro,
a heathen approached some of my men, handed them
a basket of cured fish, and said, "Thursday-Friday-Saturday-Sunday,"
in precise and impeccable Spanish.

Where he learned this is yet to be known. It is very strange,
of course, and troubling, for these people know almost nothing of God
and have absolutely no need for days.

El Camino Real 3

We're balancing the heat of the day
on the tops of our heads, walking
along the shoulder of the road
to the new liquor store for Cokes,
which she said would take fifteen minutes tops
but instead is taking over an hour.
On one side, a field of cotton, ready
to be picked, thick and white
with loosened bulbs; on the other, hard dirt
and nothing, then a ditch, a road, some
morbid-looking piece of farming equipment,
and in the distance, the rise of the interstate
and the woozy sound it makes.
In loose reference to a conversation
we've been having off and on all summer,
she says, "Okay, what if we're already dead
and this is heaven?" The question hangs there
in front of us. We walk through it. A car
passes us from behind, and the hot breeze
hits the backs of our legs. The road curves.
Far ahead, the liquor store flashes
its bottles of booze. "We're here," she sings,
though we're not there and won't be there
for another ten minutes. Between us
and the store, the road waves its fingers
of heat. Beyond the store, the road gets thin
but doesn't disappear. As far as we know,
it goes on forever.

PENGUIN POETS

JOHN ASHBERY
Selected Poems
Self-Portrait in a Convex Mirror

TED BERRIGAN
The Sonnets

JOE BONOMO
Installations

PHILIP BOOTH
Selves

JIM CARROLL
Fear of Dreaming: The Selected
  Poems
Living at the Movies
Void of Course

ALISON HAWTHORNE
DEMING
Genius Loci
Rope

CARL DENNIS
New and Selected Poems, 1974–2004
Practical Gods
Ranking the Wishes
Unknown Friends

DIANE DI PRIMA
Loba

STUART DISCHELL
Backwards Days
Dig Safe

STEPHEN DOBYNS
Velocities: New and Selected Poems,
  1966–1992

EDWARD DORN
Way More West: New and Selected
  Poems

AMY GERSTLER
Crown of Weeds: Poems
Dearest Creature
Ghost Girl
Medicine
Nerve Storm

EUGENE GLORIA
Drivers at the Short-Time Motel
Hoodlum Birds

DEBORA GREGER
Desert Fathers, Uranium Daughters
God

Men, Women, and Ghosts
Western Art

TERRANCE HAYES
Hip Logic
Lighthead
Wind in a Box

ROBERT HUNTER
Sentinel and Other Poems

MARY KARR
Viper Rum

WILLIAM KECKLER
Sanskrit of the Body

JACK KEROUAC
Book of Sketches
Book of Blues
Book of Haikus

JOANNA KLINK
Circadian
Raptus

JOANNE KYGER
As Ever: Selected Poems

ANN LAUTERBACH
Hum
If In Time: Selected Poems, 1975–
  2000
On a Stair
Or to Begin Again

CORINNE LEE
PYX

PHILLIS LEVIN
May Day
Mercury

WILLIAM LOGAN
Macbeth in Venice
Strange Flesh
The Whispering Gallery

ADRIAN MATEJKA
Mixology

MICHAEL MCCLURE
Huge Dreams: San Francisco and
  Beat Poems

DAVID MELTZER
David's Copy: The Selected Poems
  of David Meltzer

CAROL MUSKE
An Octave above Thunder
Red Trousseau

ALICE NOTLEY
The Descent of Alette
Disobedience
In the Pines
Mysteries of Small Houses

LAWRENCE RAAB
The History of Forgetting
Visible Signs: New and Selected
  Poems

BARBARA RAS
The Last Skin
One Hidden Stuff

PATTIANN ROGERS
Generations
Wayfare

WILLIAM STOBB
Nervous Systems

TRYFON TOLIDES
An Almost Pure Empty Walking

ANNE WALDMAN
Kill or Cure
Manatee/Humanity
Structure of the World Compared
  to a Bubble

JAMES WELCH
Riding the Earthboy 40

PHILIP WHALEN
Overtime: Selected Poems

ROBERT WRIGLEY
Earthly Meditations: New and
  Selected Poems
Lives of the Animals
Reign of Snakes

MARK YAKICH
The Importance of Peeling
  Potatoes in Ukraine
Unrelated Individuals Forming a
  Group Waiting to Cross

JOHN YAU
Borrowed Love Poems
Paradiso Diaspora

Printed in the United States
by Baker & Taylor Publisher Services